8 SEAS⬥NS
of my week

☑ Weekly Planner   ☑ Task Manager   ☑ Productivity Tool

KAI NORTHCOTT

Welcome to 8 Seasons!

This is your weekly planner, task manager and productivity tool.

Structuring our time can be hard, and this book is designed to make it easier. If you struggle with long task lists, knowing when to do what, or getting started when there's no time pressure, this book is for you. You can map out your days, weeks and work sessions using the 8 Seasons System, or whatever flow works for you.

Each week gets two 2-page spreads: one for **goals, inspirations and other notes**, and one for mapping out the activities of your days, weeks and work sessions. First let's look at the pages for notes, and then get into the week maps.

At the very top: **Goals** for the week. I recommend choosing your top three goals for the week, and you've got enough space to write in more than three.

Next, **Things I've noticed inside** and **Things I've noticed outside.** Those could be things you've seen, felt, or experienced inside your home / outside your home, inside your self / outside your self, or any other inside/outside that fits you better.

At the bottom of the left page is a section to record especially beautiful things about your day (**roses**), things you see developing and blossoming (**buds**), and the painful parts of your day (**thorns**).

At the top of the right page you have space to write down those

Inspirations / Big Ideas that hit you in the middle of the night, when you're working on another project, or whenever they strike you. Keep coming back to these as the weeks go by, and see which inspirations you want to transform into goals.

A huge purpose of this book is to help you schedule your tasks, so you can use the **Unscheduled Tasks** section as a holding place while you figure out where to map those tasks in your week.

Opportunities to Connect could be with yourself, with others or with nature. Personal, professional or community. For work or for fun. With purpose or just because. We all need more connection in our lives, and here's where you can track and plan a little more into your life.

And at the very bottom of that page is a space to write your **intention for the day**, an **affirmation for the day**, or just something you observed about the day. If you've tried affirmations and when you do a voice in your head tries to disagree about all the positive things you're telling yourself... One, you're not alone. That happens to me too, so I don't use affirmations. Instead, I transform that affirmation into an **IFfirmation** by making into a question: "What IF I have good habits?" "What IF I keep my commitments?" "What IF I take good care of myself?" with So you can use that section to write those questions and/or any answers that come to your mind. Or simply note something you observed about your day.

All those notes will help you track some essential info, and get ready to map out your weeks. So let's get into those week maps.

For this week map concept to make sense, we first need to establish that each day and each year are divided into **8 phases**, each of which has a certain energy to it. Those 8 Seasons establish an energetic archetype that looks like this:

NE	Magic, transition
E	Inspiration
SE	Preparation
S	Focus, work
SW	Self-care
W	Connection
NW	Reflection
N	The Big Vision

Your day is divided similarly, but the phases of your day don't have to line up with the timing of the natural day. Your NE starts when you wake up, no matter what time it is, and you move through each phase of the day from there, until you get ready for bed in the NW and sleep in the N (again, no matter what time it is). So your day looks like this:

NE	Waking up your mind & spirit
E	Waking up your body
SE	Preparing for the day's mission
S	The Mission
SW	Resting and recovering
W	Connecting
NW	Winding down, getting ready for bed
N	Rest

In this book I give the South of your day it's own wheel, so you can map out your work session for maximum effectiveness. The wheel of your work session looks like this:

NE	Conscious opening
E	Get inspired
SE	Prepare
S	Focused work
SW	Break for self-care
W	Connections
NW	Reviewing today, planning tomorrow
N	Orient to the vision
NE	Conscious closing

Your week also has **8 phases** to it, and those look like this:

NE	Time off, R&R
E	Look ahead, get inspired
SE	Plan and prepare
S	Do the work
SW	Self-care
W	Connection
NW	Reflecting, planning
N	Orient to the vision

You may find that you move through several phases of your week in one day, or that some phases of your week span multiple days. I generally aim to complete my E & SE on Monday, and let my S span Tuesday and Wednesday. And in the future I hope to create a life where NE spans 4 days, and I rock out E through NW on Tuesday, Wednesday and Thursday. You get to decide how long each phase of your week is, and what day(s) they happen on. The important part is to move through the phases of your week in order.

So hopefully by now you see that these three wheels interlock to create wheels within wheels within wheels. And you can begin to see how to use that to map out your activities for the week. You might map out your week in the S of the work session in the SE phase of your week. You might schedule your meetings for the S or W of the work session in the W phase of your week, and plan the agendas for those meetings in the SE of your W.

All that making sense?

For more ideas on how to use this book, you can find a series of short videos in the "How to use my books" playlist at **www.tiktok.com/ @kai8seasons**

To learn more about me and my coaching practice, check out **www.8seasons.consulting**

And if you're ready for personalized support implementing the principles of this book, you can book a free call with me at **www.KaiNorthcott.as.me**

Blessing on your journey of structuring your time and managing your energy. I'll talk to you soon.

Kai

Goals

1

2

3

ROSES

BUDS

THORNS

▼ INSPIRATIONS / BIG IDEAS

_____ WEEK OF _____

▼ UNSCHEDULED TASKS

▼ OPPORTUNITIES TO CONNECT

▼ INTENTION / AFFIRMATION / IFFIRMATION / OBSERVATION

NE

E

SE

ne

e

se

S

sw

w

nw

n

ne

SW

W

NW

N

DAY _____   _____ DAY _____   _____ DAY _____   _____ DAY _____

NE

E

SE

ne

e

se

S

sw

w

nw

n

ne

SW

W

NW

N

Goals

1

2

3

▼ **THINGS I'VE NOTICED INSIDE**

▼ **THINGS I'VE NOTICED OUTSIDE**

ROSES

BUDS

THORNS

▼ INSPIRATIONS / BIG IDEAS

_____ WEEK OF _____

▼ UNSCHEDULED TASKS

▼ OPPORTUNITIES TO CONNECT

▼ INTENTION / AFFIRMATION / IFFIRMATION / OBSERVATION

DAY _____   _____ DAY _____   _____ DAY_____   _____

NE

E

SE

ne

e

se

S

sw

w

nw

n

ne

SW

W

NW

N

DAY _____   _____ DAY _____   _____ DAY _____   _____ DAY _____

NE

E

SE

ne

e

se

S

sw

w

nw

n

ne

SW

W

NW

N

Goals

1

2

3

▼ THINGS I'VE NOTICED INSIDE

▼ THINGS I'VE NOTICED OUTSIDE

ROSES

BUDS

THORNS

▼ INSPIRATIONS / BIG IDEAS

_____ WEEK OF _____

▼ UNSCHEDULED TASKS

▼ OPPORTUNITIES TO CONNECT

▼ INTENTION / AFFIRMATION / IFFIRMATION / OBSERVATION

DAY _____ DAY _____ DAY _____ _____

NE

E

SE

ne

e

se

S

sw

w

nw

n

ne

SW

W

NW

N

DAY _____   _____ DAY _____   _____ DAY _____   _____ DAY _____

NE

E

SE

ne

e

se

S

sw

w

nw

n

ne

SW

W

NW

N

Goals

1

2

3

▼ THINGS I'VE NOTICED INSIDE

▼ THINGS I'VE NOTICED OUTSIDE

ROSES

BUDS

THORNS

▼ INSPIRATIONS / BIG IDEAS

▼ UNSCHEDULED TASKS

▼ OPPORTUNITIES TO CONNECT

▼ INTENTION / AFFIRMATION / IFFIRMATION / OBSERVATION

_____ **DAY** _____   _____ **DAY** _____   _____ **DAY** _____   _____

NE

E

SE

ne

e

se

S

sw

w

nw

n

ne

SW

W

NW

N

DAY ___ ___ ___ DAY ___ ___ ___ DAY ___ ___ ___ DAY ___

WEEK
OF

___

NE

E

SE

ne

e

se

S

sw

w

nw

n

ne

SW

W

NW

N

Goals

1

2

3

▼ **THINGS I'VE NOTICED INSIDE**

▼ **THINGS I'VE NOTICED OUTSIDE**

ROSES	BUDS	THORNS

▼ INSPIRATIONS / BIG IDEAS

▼ WEEK OF

▼ UNSCHEDULED TASKS

▼ OPPORTUNITIES TO CONNECT

▼ INTENTION / AFFIRMATION / IFFIRMATION / OBSERVATION

NE

E

SE

ne

e

se

S

sw

w

nw

n

ne

SW

W

NW

N

DAY _____ _____ DAY _____ _____ DAY _____ _____ DAY _____

NE

E

SE

ne

e

se

S

sw

w

nw

n

ne

SW

W

NW

N

Goals

1

2

3

▼ THINGS I'VE NOTICED INSIDE

▼ THINGS I'VE NOTICED OUTSIDE

ROSES

BUDS

THORNS

▼ INSPIRATIONS / BIG IDEAS   _____ WEEK OF _____

▼ UNSCHEDULED TASKS   ▼ OPPORTUNITIES TO CONNECT

▼ INTENTION / AFFIRMATION / IFFIRMATION / OBSERVATION

NE

E

SE

ne

e

se

S

sw

w

nw

n

ne

SW

W

NW

N

DAY _____   _____ DAY _____   _____ DAY _____   _____ DAY _____

Goals

1

2

3

▼ THINGS I'VE NOTICED INSIDE

▼ THINGS I'VE NOTICED OUTSIDE

ROSES

BUDS

THORNS

▼ INSPIRATIONS / BIG IDEAS

_____ WEEK OF _____

▼ UNSCHEDULED TASKS

▼ OPPORTUNITIES TO CONNECT

▼ INTENTION / AFFIRMATION / IFFIRMATION / OBSERVATION

NE

E

SE

ne

e

se

S

sw

w

nw

n

ne

SW

W

NW

N

DAY _____   _____ DAY _____   _____ DAY _____   _____ DAY _____

WEEK
OF

NE

E

SE

ne

e

se

S

sw

w

nw

n

ne

SW

W

NW

N

Goals

1

2

3

▼ THINGS I'VE NOTICED INSIDE

▼ THINGS I'VE NOTICED OUTSIDE

ROSES

BUDS

THORNS

▼ INSPIRATIONS / BIG IDEAS

▼ UNSCHEDULED TASKS

▼ OPPORTUNITIES TO CONNECT

▼ INTENTION / AFFIRMATION / IFFIRMATION / OBSERVATION

NE

E

SE

ne

e

se

S

sw

w

nw

n

ne

SW

W

NW

N

DAY _____   _____ DAY _____   _____ DAY _____   _____ DAY _____

NE

E

SE

ne

e

se

S

sw

w

nw

n

ne

SW

W

NW

N

Goals

1

2

3

▼ THINGS I'VE NOTICED INSIDE

▼ THINGS I'VE NOTICED OUTSIDE

| ROSES | BUDS | THORNS |

▼ INSPIRATIONS / BIG IDEAS

_____ WEEK OF _____

▼ UNSCHEDULED TASKS

▼ OPPORTUNITIES TO CONNECT

▼ INTENTION / AFFIRMATION / IFFIRMATION / OBSERVATION

NE

E

SE

ne

e

se

S

sw

w

nw

n

ne

SW

W

NW

N

DAY _____ _____ DAY _____ _____ DAY _____ _____ DAY _____

_____

NE

E

SE

ne

e

se

S

sw

w

nw

n

ne

SW

W

NW

N

Goals

1

2

3

▼ THINGS I'VE NOTICED INSIDE

▼ THINGS I'VE NOTICED OUTSIDE

ROSES

BUDS

THORNS

▼ INSPIRATIONS / BIG IDEAS

_____ WEEK OF _____

▼ UNSCHEDULED TASKS

▼ OPPORTUNITIES TO CONNECT

▼ INTENTION / AFFIRMATION / IFFIRMATION / OBSERVATION

NE

E

SE

ne

e

se

S

sw

w

nw

n

ne

SW

W

NW

N

DAY _____ _____ DAY _____ _____ DAY _____ _____ DAY _____

NE

E

SE

ne

e

se

S

sw

w

nw

n

ne

SW

W

NW

N

Goals

1

2

3

▼ THINGS I'VE NOTICED INSIDE

▼ THINGS I'VE NOTICED OUTSIDE

ROSES

BUDS

THORNS

▼ INSPIRATIONS / BIG IDEAS

_____ WEEK OF _____

▼ UNSCHEDULED TASKS

▼ OPPORTUNITIES TO CONNECT

▼ INTENTION / AFFIRMATION / IFFIRMATION / OBSERVATION

NE

E

SE

ne

e

se

S

sw

w

nw

n

ne

SW

W

NW

N

DAY _____ _____ DAY _____ _____ DAY _____ _____ DAY _____

_____

NE

E

SE

ne

e

se

S

sw

w

nw

n

ne

SW

W

NW

N

Goals

1

2

3

▼ THINGS I'VE NOTICED INSIDE

▼ THINGS I'VE NOTICED OUTSIDE

ROSES

BUDS

THORNS

▼ INSPIRATIONS / BIG IDEAS

_____ WEEK OF _____

▼ UNSCHEDULED TASKS

▼ OPPORTUNITIES TO CONNECT

▼ INTENTION / AFFIRMATION / IFFIRMATION / OBSERVATION

_____ DAY _____   _____ DAY _____   _____ DAY _____   _____

NE

E

SE

ne

e

se

S

sw

w

nw

n

ne

SW

W

NW

N

DAY ____ ____ DAY ____ ____ DAY ____ ____ DAY ____

WEEK
OF
____

NE

E

SE

ne

e

se

S

sw

w

nw

n

ne

SW

W

NW

N

Goals

1

2

3

▼ THINGS I'VE NOTICED INSIDE

▼ THINGS I'VE NOTICED OUTSIDE

ROSES

BUDS

THORNS

▼ INSPIRATIONS / BIG IDEAS

▼ UNSCHEDULED TASKS

▼ OPPORTUNITIES TO CONNECT

▼ INTENTION / AFFIRMATION / IFFIRMATION / OBSERVATION

NE

E

SE

ne

e

se

S

sw

w

nw

n

ne

SW

W

NW

N

DAY _____ _____ DAY _____ _____ DAY _____ _____ DAY _____

WEEK OF
_____

NE

E

SE

ne

e

se

S

sw

w

nw

n

ne

SW

W

NW

N

Goals

1

2

3

▼ THINGS I'VE NOTICED INSIDE

▼ THINGS I'VE NOTICED OUTSIDE

ROSES

BUDS

THORNS

▼ INSPIRATIONS / BIG IDEAS

_____ WEEK OF _____

▼ UNSCHEDULED TASKS

▼ OPPORTUNITIES TO CONNECT

▼ INTENTION / AFFIRMATION / IFFIRMATION / OBSERVATION

_____ DAY _____   _____ DAY _____   _____ DAY _____   _____

NE

E

SE

ne

e

se

S

sw

w

nw

n

ne

SW

W

NW

N

DAY _____ _____ DAY _____ _____ DAY _____ _____ DAY _____

Goals

1

2

3

▼ THINGS I'VE NOTICED INSIDE

▼ THINGS I'VE NOTICED OUTSIDE

ROSES

BUDS

THORNS

▼ INSPIRATIONS / BIG IDEAS

▼ UNSCHEDULED TASKS

▼ OPPORTUNITIES TO CONNECT

▼ INTENTION / AFFIRMATION / IFFIRMATION / OBSERVATION

NE

E

SE

ne

e

se

S

sw

w

nw

n

ne

SW

W

NW

N

DAY ____ _____ DAY ____ _____ DAY ____ _____ DAY ____

____

NE

E

SE

ne

e

se

S

sw

w

nw

n

ne

SW

W

NW

N

Goals

1

2

3

▼ **THINGS I'VE NOTICED INSIDE**

▼ **THINGS I'VE NOTICED OUTSIDE**

ROSES

BUDS

THORNS

▼ INSPIRATIONS / BIG IDEAS

▼ UNSCHEDULED TASKS

▼ OPPORTUNITIES TO CONNECT

▼ INTENTION / AFFIRMATION / IFFIRMATION / OBSERVATION

NE

E

SE

ne

e

se

S

sw

w

nw

n

ne

SW

W

NW

N

DAY _____ _____ DAY _____ _____ DAY _____ _____ DAY _____

Goals

1

2

3

▼ THINGS I'VE NOTICED INSIDE

▼ THINGS I'VE NOTICED OUTSIDE

ROSES

BUDS

THORNS

▼ INSPIRATIONS / BIG IDEAS

_____ WEEK OF _____

▼ UNSCHEDULED TASKS

▼ OPPORTUNITIES TO CONNECT

▼ INTENTION / AFFIRMATION / IFFIRMATION / OBSERVATION

NE

E

SE

ne

e

se

S

sw

w

nw

n

ne

SW

W

NW

N

DAY _____   _____ DAY _____   _____ DAY _____   _____ DAY _____

NE

E

SE

ne

e

se

S

sw

w

nw

n

ne

SW

W

NW

N

Goals

1

2

3

▼ **THINGS I'VE NOTICED INSIDE**

▼ **THINGS I'VE NOTICED OUTSIDE**

ROSES

BUDS

THORNS

▼ INSPIRATIONS / BIG IDEAS

▼ UNSCHEDULED TASKS

▼ OPPORTUNITIES TO CONNECT

▼ INTENTION / AFFIRMATION / IFFIRMATION / OBSERVATION

NE

E

SE

ne

e

se

S

sw

w

nw

n

ne

SW

W

NW

N

DAY _____ _____ DAY _____ _____ DAY _____ _____ DAY _____

NE

E

SE

ne

e

se

S

sw

w

nw

n

ne

SW

W

NW

N

Goals

1

2

3

▼ THINGS I'VE NOTICED INSIDE

▼ THINGS I'VE NOTICED OUTSIDE

ROSES

BUDS

THORNS

▼ INSPIRATIONS / BIG IDEAS

_____ WEEK OF _____

▼ UNSCHEDULED TASKS

▼ OPPORTUNITIES TO CONNECT

▼ INTENTION / AFFIRMATION / IFFIRMATION / OBSERVATION

NE

E

SE

ne

e

se

S

sw

w

nw

n

ne

SW

W

NW

N

DAY _____ _____ DAY _____ _____ DAY _____ _____ DAY _____

WEEK
OF
_____

NE

E

SE

ne

e

se

S

sw

w

nw

n

ne

SW

W

NW

N

Goals

1

2

3

▼ **THINGS I'VE NOTICED INSIDE**

▼ **THINGS I'VE NOTICED OUTSIDE**

| ROSES | BUDS | THORNS |

▼ INSPIRATIONS / BIG IDEAS

_____ WEEK OF _____

▼ UNSCHEDULED TASKS

▼ OPPORTUNITIES TO CONNECT

▼ INTENTION / AFFIRMATION / IFFIRMATION / OBSERVATION

_____DAY_____   _____DAY_____   _____DAY_____   _____

NE

E

SE

ne

e

se

S

sw

w

nw

n

ne

SW

W

NW

N

DAY _____ _____ DAY _____ _____ DAY _____ _____ DAY _____

Goals

1

2

3

▼ **THINGS I'VE NOTICED INSIDE**

▼ **THINGS I'VE NOTICED OUTSIDE**

ROSES

BUDS

THORNS

▼ INSPIRATIONS / BIG IDEAS

▼ UNSCHEDULED TASKS

▼ OPPORTUNITIES TO CONNECT

▼ INTENTION / AFFIRMATION / IFFIRMATION / OBSERVATION

_____ DAY _____   _____ DAY _____   _____ DAY _____   _____

NE

E

SE

ne

e

se

S

sw

w

nw

n

ne

SW

W

NW

N

DAY____ _____DAY____ _____DAY____ _____DAY____

NE

E

SE

ne

e

se

S

sw

w

nw

n

ne

SW

W

NW

N

Goals

1

2

3

▼ THINGS I'VE NOTICED INSIDE

▼ THINGS I'VE NOTICED OUTSIDE

ROSES

BUDS

THORNS

▼ INSPIRATIONS / BIG IDEAS

▼ UNSCHEDULED TASKS

▼ OPPORTUNITIES TO CONNECT

▼ INTENTION / AFFIRMATION / IFFIRMATION / OBSERVATION

_____ DAY _____   _____ DAY _____   _____ DAY _____   _____

NE

E

SE

ne

e

se

S

sw

w

nw

n

ne

SW

W

NW

N

DAY _____   _____ DAY _____   _____ DAY _____   _____ DAY _____

NE

E

SE

ne

e

se

S

sw

w

nw

n

ne

SW

W

NW

N

Goals

1

2

3

▼ THINGS I'VE NOTICED INSIDE

▼ THINGS I'VE NOTICED OUTSIDE

ROSES

BUDS

THORNS

▼ INSPIRATIONS / BIG IDEAS

_____ WEEK OF _____

▼ UNSCHEDULED TASKS

▼ OPPORTUNITIES TO CONNECT

▼ INTENTION / AFFIRMATION / IFFIRMATION / OBSERVATION

_____ DAY _____   _____ DAY _____   _____ DAY _____   _____

NE

E

SE

ne

e

se

S

sw

w

nw

n

ne

SW

W

NW

N

WEEK
OF
_____

DAY _____ _____ DAY _____ _____ DAY _____ _____ DAY _____

NE

E

SE

ne

e

se

S

sw

w

nw

n

ne

SW

W

NW

N

Goals

1

2

3

▼ THINGS I'VE NOTICED INSIDE

▼ THINGS I'VE NOTICED OUTSIDE

ROSES	BUDS	THORNS

▼ INSPIRATIONS / BIG IDEAS

▼ UNSCHEDULED TASKS

▼ OPPORTUNITIES TO CONNECT

▼ INTENTION / AFFIRMATION / IFFIRMATION / OBSERVATION

	DAY	DAY	DAY	
NE				
E				
SE				
ne				
e				
se				
S				
sw				
w				
nw				
n				
ne				
SW				
W				
NW				
N				

DAY _____   _____ DAY _____   _____ DAY _____   _____ DAY _____

_____

NE

E

SE

ne

e

se

S

sw

w

nw

n

ne

SW

W

NW

N

Goals

1

2

3

▼ THINGS I'VE NOTICED INSIDE

▼ THINGS I'VE NOTICED OUTSIDE

ROSES

BUDS

THORNS

▼ INSPIRATIONS / BIG IDEAS

_____ WEEK OF _____

▼ UNSCHEDULED TASKS

▼ OPPORTUNITIES TO CONNECT

▼ INTENTION / AFFIRMATION / IFFIRMATION / OBSERVATION

NE

E

SE

ne

e

se

S

sw

w

nw

n

ne

SW

W

NW

N

DAY _____ _____ DAY _____ _____ DAY _____ _____ DAY _____

WEEK
OF

_____

NE

E

SE

ne

e

se

S

sw

w

nw

n

ne

SW

W

NW

N

Goals

1

2

3

▼ THINGS I'VE NOTICED INSIDE

▼ THINGS I'VE NOTICED OUTSIDE

ROSES

BUDS

THORNS

▼ INSPIRATIONS / BIG IDEAS

▼ UNSCHEDULED TASKS

▼ OPPORTUNITIES TO CONNECT

▼ INTENTION / AFFIRMATION / IFFIRMATION / OBSERVATION

_____DAY_____   _____DAY____   _____DAY____   _____

NE

E

SE

ne

e

se

S

sw

w

nw

n

ne

SW

W

NW

N

DAY _____ _____ DAY _____ _____ DAY _____ _____ DAY _____

_____

NE

E

SE

ne

e

se

S

sw

w

nw

n

ne

SW

W

NW

N

Goals

1

2

3

▼ THINGS I'VE NOTICED INSIDE

▼ THINGS I'VE NOTICED OUTSIDE

| ROSES | BUDS | THORNS |

▼ INSPIRATIONS / BIG IDEAS

_____ WEEK OF _____

▼ UNSCHEDULED TASKS

▼ OPPORTUNITIES TO CONNECT

▼ INTENTION / AFFIRMATION / IFFIRMATION / OBSERVATION

NE

E

SE

ne

e

se

S

sw

w

nw

n

ne

SW

W

NW

N

DAY _____   _____ **DAY** _____   _____ **DAY** _____   _____ **DAY** _____

_____

NE

E

SE

ne

e

se

S

sw

w

nw

n

ne

SW

W

NW

N

Goals

1

2

3

▼ **THINGS I'VE NOTICED INSIDE**

▼ **THINGS I'VE NOTICED OUTSIDE**

ROSES

BUDS

THORNS

▼ INSPIRATIONS / BIG IDEAS

_____ WEEK OF _____

▼ UNSCHEDULED TASKS

▼ OPPORTUNITIES TO CONNECT

▼ INTENTION / AFFIRMATION / IFFIRMATION / OBSERVATION

NE

E

SE

ne

e

se

S

sw

w

nw

n

ne

SW

W

NW

N

DAY _____ _____ DAY _____ _____ DAY _____ _____ DAY _____

NE

E

SE

ne

e

se

S

sw

w

nw

n

ne

SW

W

NW

N

Goals

1

2

3

▼ THINGS I'VE NOTICED INSIDE

▼ THINGS I'VE NOTICED OUTSIDE

ROSES

BUDS

THORNS

▼ INSPIRATIONS / BIG IDEAS

▼ UNSCHEDULED TASKS

▼ OPPORTUNITIES TO CONNECT

▼ INTENTION / AFFIRMATION / IFFIRMATION / OBSERVATION

NE

E

SE

ne

e

se

S

sw

w

nw

n

ne

SW

W

NW

N

DAY _____   _____ DAY _____   _____ DAY _____   _____ DAY _____

NE

E

SE

ne

e

se

S

sw

w

nw

n

ne

SW

W

NW

N

Goals

1

2

3

▼ THINGS I'VE NOTICED INSIDE

▼ THINGS I'VE NOTICED OUTSIDE

ROSES

BUDS

THORNS

▼ INSPIRATIONS / BIG IDEAS

_____ WEEK OF _____

▼ UNSCHEDULED TASKS

▼ OPPORTUNITIES TO CONNECT

▼ INTENTION / AFFIRMATION / IFFIRMATION / OBSERVATION

NE

E

SE

ne

e

se

S

sw

w

nw

n

ne

SW

W

NW

N

DAY _____   _____ **DAY** _____   _____ **DAY** _____   _____ **DAY** _____

_____

NE

E

SE

ne

e

se

S

sw

w

nw

n

ne

SW

W

NW

N

Goals

1

2

3

▼ **THINGS I'VE NOTICED INSIDE**

▼ **THINGS I'VE NOTICED OUTSIDE**

ROSES

BUDS

THORNS

▼ INSPIRATIONS / BIG IDEAS

_____ WEEK OF _____

▼ UNSCHEDULED TASKS

▼ OPPORTUNITIES TO CONNECT

▼ INTENTION / AFFIRMATION / IFFIRMATION / OBSERVATION

_____ DAY_____   _____ DAY_____   _____ DAY_____   _____

NE

E

SE

ne

e

se

S

sw

w

nw

n

ne

SW

W

NW

N

DAY_____   _____DAY_____   _____DAY_____   _____DAY_____

NE

E

SE

ne

e

se

S

sw

w

nw

n

ne

SW

W

NW

N

Goals

1

2

3

▼ **THINGS I'VE NOTICED INSIDE**

▼ **THINGS I'VE NOTICED OUTSIDE**

ROSES

BUDS

THORNS

▼ INSPIRATIONS / BIG IDEAS

▼ UNSCHEDULED TASKS

▼ OPPORTUNITIES TO CONNECT

▼ INTENTION / AFFIRMATION / IFFIRMATION / OBSERVATION

_____ DAY _____   _____ DAY _____   _____ DAY _____   _____

NE

E

SE

ne

e

se

S

sw

w

nw

n

ne

SW

W

NW

N

DAY _____ _____ DAY _____ _____ DAY _____ _____ DAY _____

NE

E

SE

ne

e

se

S

sw

w

nw

n

ne

SW

W

NW

N

Goals

1

2

3

▼ **THINGS I'VE NOTICED INSIDE**

▼ **THINGS I'VE NOTICED OUTSIDE**

ROSES

BUDS

THORNS

▼ INSPIRATIONS / BIG IDEAS

▼ UNSCHEDULED TASKS

▼ OPPORTUNITIES TO CONNECT

▼ INTENTION / AFFIRMATION / IFFIRMATION / OBSERVATION

NE

E

SE

ne

e

se

S

sw

w

nw

n

ne

SW

W

NW

N

DAY _____   _____ DAY _____   _____ DAY _____   _____ DAY _____

Goals

1

2

3

▼ THINGS I'VE NOTICED INSIDE

▼ THINGS I'VE NOTICED OUTSIDE

ROSES

BUDS

THORNS

▼ INSPIRATIONS / BIG IDEAS

▼ UNSCHEDULED TASKS

▼ OPPORTUNITIES TO CONNECT

▼ INTENTION / AFFIRMATION / IFFIRMATION / OBSERVATION

DAY _____ DAY _____ DAY _____ _____

NE

E

SE

ne

e

se

S

sw

w

nw

n

ne

SW

W

NW

N

DAY _____   _____ DAY _____   _____ DAY _____   _____ DAY _____

Goals

1

2

3

▼ **THINGS I'VE NOTICED INSIDE**

▼ **THINGS I'VE NOTICED OUTSIDE**

ROSES

BUDS

THORNS

▼ INSPIRATIONS / BIG IDEAS   _____ WEEK OF _____

▼ UNSCHEDULED TASKS   ▼ OPPORTUNITIES TO CONNECT

▼ INTENTION / AFFIRMATION / IFFIRMATION / OBSERVATION

_____ DAY _____   _____ DAY _____   _____ DAY _____   _____

NE

E

SE

ne

e

se

S

sw

w

nw

n

ne

SW

W

NW

N

DAY _____ _____ DAY _____ _____ DAY _____ _____ DAY _____

NE

E

SE

ne

e

se

S

sw

w

nw

n

ne

SW

W

NW

N

Goals

1

2

3

▼ THINGS I'VE NOTICED INSIDE

▼ THINGS I'VE NOTICED OUTSIDE

ROSES

BUDS

THORNS

▼ INSPIRATIONS / BIG IDEAS

_____ WEEK OF _____

▼ UNSCHEDULED TASKS

▼ OPPORTUNITIES TO CONNECT

▼ INTENTION / AFFIRMATION / IFFIRMATION / OBSERVATION

NE

E

SE

ne

e

se

S

sw

w

nw

n

ne

SW

W

NW

N

DAY _____ _____ DAY _____ _____ DAY _____ _____ DAY _____

_____

NE

E

SE

ne

e

se

S

sw

w

nw

n

ne

SW

W

NW

N

Goals

1

2

3

▼ THINGS I'VE NOTICED INSIDE

▼ THINGS I'VE NOTICED OUTSIDE

ROSES

BUDS

THORNS

▼ INSPIRATIONS / BIG IDEAS

_____ WEEK OF _____

▼ UNSCHEDULED TASKS

▼ OPPORTUNITIES TO CONNECT

▼ INTENTION / AFFIRMATION / IFFIRMATION / OBSERVATION

NE

E

SE

ne

e

se

S

sw

w

nw

n

ne

SW

W

NW

N

DAY_____   _____DAY_____   _____DAY_____   _____DAY_____

_____

NE

E

SE

ne

e

se

S

sw

w

nw

n

ne

SW

W

NW

N

Goals

1

2

3

▼ THINGS I'VE NOTICED INSIDE

▼ THINGS I'VE NOTICED OUTSIDE

ROSES

BUDS

THORNS

▼ INSPIRATIONS / BIG IDEAS

_____ WEEK OF _____

▼ UNSCHEDULED TASKS

▼ OPPORTUNITIES TO CONNECT

▼ INTENTION / AFFIRMATION / IFFIRMATION / OBSERVATION

NE

E

SE

ne

e

se

S

sw

w

nw

n

ne

SW

W

NW

N

DAY _____   _____ DAY _____   _____ DAY _____   _____ DAY _____

NE

E

SE

ne

e

se

S

sw

w

nw

n

ne

SW

W

NW

N

Goals

1

2

3

▼ **THINGS I'VE NOTICED INSIDE**

▼ **THINGS I'VE NOTICED OUTSIDE**

ROSES

BUDS

THORNS

▼ INSPIRATIONS / BIG IDEAS

WEEK OF

▼ UNSCHEDULED TASKS

▼ OPPORTUNITIES TO CONNECT

▼ INTENTION / AFFIRMATION / IFFIRMATION / OBSERVATION

NE

E

SE

ne

e

se

S

sw

w

nw

n

ne

SW

W

NW

N

DAY _____   _____ DAY _____   _____ DAY _____   _____ DAY _____

NE

E

SE

ne

e

se

S

sw

w

nw

n

ne

SW

W

NW

N

Goals

1

2

3

▼ THINGS I'VE NOTICED INSIDE

▼ THINGS I'VE NOTICED OUTSIDE

ROSES	BUDS	THORNS

▼ INSPIRATIONS / BIG IDEAS

_____ WEEK OF _____

▼ UNSCHEDULED TASKS

▼ OPPORTUNITIES TO CONNECT

▼ INTENTION / AFFIRMATION / IFFIRMATION / OBSERVATION

NE

E

SE

ne

e

se

S

sw

w

nw

n

ne

SW

W

NW

N

DAY _____   _____ DAY _____   _____ DAY _____   _____ DAY _____

NE

E

SE

ne

e

se

S

sw

w

nw

n

ne

SW

W

NW

N

Goals

1

2

3

▼ THINGS I'VE NOTICED INSIDE

▼ THINGS I'VE NOTICED OUTSIDE

ROSES

BUDS

THORNS

▼ INSPIRATIONS / BIG IDEAS   _____ WEEK OF _____

▼ UNSCHEDULED TASKS   ▼ OPPORTUNITIES TO CONNECT

▼ INTENTION / AFFIRMATION / IFFIRMATION / OBSERVATION

NE

E

SE

ne

e

se

S

sw

w

nw

n

ne

SW

W

NW

N

DAY_____   _____DAY_____   _____DAY_____   _____DAY_____

NE

E

SE

ne

e

se

S

sw

w

nw

n

ne

SW

W

NW

N

Goals

1

2

3

▼ **THINGS I'VE NOTICED INSIDE**

▼ **THINGS I'VE NOTICED OUTSIDE**

ROSES

BUDS

THORNS

▼ INSPIRATIONS / BIG IDEAS

_____ WEEK OF _____

▼ UNSCHEDULED TASKS

▼ OPPORTUNITIES TO CONNECT

▼ INTENTION / AFFIRMATION / IFFIRMATION / OBSERVATION

DAY _____   DAY _____   DAY _____   _____

NE

E

SE

ne

e

se

S

sw

w

nw

n

ne

SW

W

NW

N

DAY_____ _____DAY_____ _____DAY_____ _____DAY_____

_____

NE

E

SE

ne

e

se

S

sw

w

nw

n

ne

SW

W

NW

N

Goals

1

2

3

▼ **THINGS I'VE NOTICED INSIDE**

▼ **THINGS I'VE NOTICED OUTSIDE**

ROSES

BUDS

THORNS

▼ INSPIRATIONS / BIG IDEAS

WEEK OF _____

▼ UNSCHEDULED TASKS

▼ OPPORTUNITIES TO CONNECT

▼ INTENTION / AFFIRMATION / IFFIRMATION / OBSERVATION

NE

E

SE

ne

e

se

S

sw

w

nw

n

ne

SW

W

NW

N

DAY _____   _____ DAY _____   _____ DAY _____   _____ DAY _____

NE

E

SE

ne

e

se

S

sw

w

nw

n

ne

SW

W

NW

N

Goals

1

2

3

▼ THINGS I'VE NOTICED INSIDE

▼ THINGS I'VE NOTICED OUTSIDE

ROSES

BUDS

THORNS

▼ INSPIRATIONS / BIG IDEAS
_____ WEEK OF _____

▼ UNSCHEDULED TASKS

▼ OPPORTUNITIES TO CONNECT

▼ INTENTION / AFFIRMATION / IFFIRMATION / OBSERVATION

NE

E

SE

ne

e

se

S

sw

w

nw

n

ne

SW

W

NW

N

DAY _____   _____ DAY _____   _____ DAY _____   _____ DAY _____   _____

NE

E

SE

ne

e

se

S

sw

w

nw

n

ne

SW

W

NW

N

Goals

1

2

3

▼ THINGS I'VE NOTICED INSIDE

▼ THINGS I'VE NOTICED OUTSIDE

ROSES

BUDS

THORNS

▼ INSPIRATIONS / BIG IDEAS

_____ WEEK OF _____

▼ UNSCHEDULED TASKS

▼ OPPORTUNITIES TO CONNECT

▼ INTENTION / AFFIRMATION / IFFIRMATION / OBSERVATION

_____DAY_____   _____DAY_____   _____DAY_____   _____

NE

E

SE

ne

e

se

S

sw

w

nw

n

ne

SW

W

NW

N

DAY _____   _____ DAY _____   _____ DAY _____   _____ DAY _____

NE

E

SE

ne

e

se

S

sw

w

nw

n

ne

SW

W

NW

N

Goals

1

2

3

▼ THINGS I'VE NOTICED INSIDE

▼ THINGS I'VE NOTICED OUTSIDE

ROSES

BUDS

THORNS

▼ INSPIRATIONS / BIG IDEAS

_____ WEEK OF _____

▼ UNSCHEDULED TASKS

▼ OPPORTUNITIES TO CONNECT

▼ INTENTION / AFFIRMATION / IFFIRMATION / OBSERVATION

_____ DAY ____   _____ DAY ____   _____ DAY ____   _____

NE

E

SE

ne

e

se

S

sw

w

nw

n

ne

SW

W

NW

N

DAY _____ _____ DAY _____ _____ DAY _____ _____ DAY _____ _____

NE

E

SE

ne

e

se

S

sw

w

nw

n

ne

SW

W

NW

N

Goals

1

2

3

▼ THINGS I'VE NOTICED INSIDE

▼ THINGS I'VE NOTICED OUTSIDE

ROSES

BUDS

THORNS

▼ INSPIRATIONS / BIG IDEAS

_____ WEEK OF _____

▼ UNSCHEDULED TASKS

▼ OPPORTUNITIES TO CONNECT

▼ INTENTION / AFFIRMATION / IFFIRMATION / OBSERVATION

NE

E

SE

ne

e

se

S

sw

w

nw

n

ne

SW

W

NW

N

DAY _____   _____ DAY _____   _____ DAY _____   _____ DAY _____

NE

E

SE

ne

e

se

S

sw

w

nw

n

ne

SW

W

NW

N

Goals

1

2

3

▼ THINGS I'VE NOTICED INSIDE

▼ THINGS I'VE NOTICED OUTSIDE

ROSES	BUDS	THORNS

▼ INSPIRATIONS / BIG IDEAS

_____ WEEK OF _____

▼ UNSCHEDULED TASKS

▼ OPPORTUNITIES TO CONNECT

▼ INTENTION / AFFIRMATION / IFFIRMATION / OBSERVATION

NE

E

SE

ne

e

se

S

sw

w

nw

n

ne

SW

W

NW

N

DAY _____   _____ DAY _____   _____ DAY _____   _____ DAY _____

NE

E

SE

ne

e

se

S

sw

w

nw

n

ne

SW

W

NW

N

Goals

1

2

3

▼ THINGS I'VE NOTICED INSIDE

▼ THINGS I'VE NOTICED OUTSIDE

ROSES

BUDS

THORNS

▼ INSPIRATIONS / BIG IDEAS

WEEK OF

▼ UNSCHEDULED TASKS

▼ OPPORTUNITIES TO CONNECT

▼ INTENTION / AFFIRMATION / IFFIRMATION / OBSERVATION

NE

E

SE

ne

e

se

S

sw

w

nw

n

ne

SW

W

NW

N

DAY ___   ___ DAY ___   ___ DAY ___   ___ DAY ___

NE

E

SE

ne

e

se

S

sw

w

nw

n

ne

SW

W

NW

N

Goals

1

2

3

▼ **THINGS I'VE NOTICED INSIDE**

▼ **THINGS I'VE NOTICED OUTSIDE**

ROSES

BUDS

THORNS

▼ INSPIRATIONS / BIG IDEAS

_____ WEEK OF _____

▼ UNSCHEDULED TASKS

▼ OPPORTUNITIES TO CONNECT

▼ INTENTION / AFFIRMATION / IFFIRMATION / OBSERVATION

NE

E

SE

ne

e

se

S

sw

w

nw

n

ne

SW

W

NW

N

DAY_____   _____DAY_____   _____DAY_____   _____DAY_____

_____

NE

E

SE

ne

e

se

S

sw

w

nw

n

ne

SW

W

NW

N

Goals

1

2

3

▼ **THINGS I'VE NOTICED INSIDE**

▼ **THINGS I'VE NOTICED OUTSIDE**

ROSES

BUDS

THORNS

▼ INSPIRATIONS / BIG IDEAS   _____ WEEK OF _____

▼ UNSCHEDULED TASKS   ▼ OPPORTUNITIES TO CONNECT

▼ INTENTION / AFFIRMATION / IFFIRMATION / OBSERVATION

NE

E

SE

ne

e

se

S

sw

w

nw

n

ne

SW

W

NW

N

DAY_____ _____**DAY**_____ _____**DAY**_____ _____**DAY**_____

NE

E

SE

ne

e

se

S

sw

w

nw

n

ne

SW

W

NW

N

Goals

1

2

3

▼ THINGS I'VE NOTICED INSIDE

▼ THINGS I'VE NOTICED OUTSIDE

ROSES	BUDS	THORNS

▼ INSPIRATIONS / BIG IDEAS   _____ WEEK OF _____

▼ UNSCHEDULED TASKS   ▼ OPPORTUNITIES TO CONNECT

▼ INTENTION / AFFIRMATION / IFFIRMATION / OBSERVATION

_____ DAY _____   _____ DAY _____   _____ DAY _____   _____

NE

E

SE

ne

e

se

S

sw

w

nw

n

ne

SW

W

NW

N

DAY _____   _____ DAY _____   _____ DAY _____   _____ DAY _____

NE

E

SE

ne

e

se

S

sw

w

nw

n

ne

SW

W

NW

N